The Real Internet of Things

The Real Internet of Things

...

Daniel Miessler

ISBN: 1545327122
ISBN 13: 9781545327128

Table of Contents

Acknowledgments

THANKS TO SAŠA ZDJELAR, ANDREW Ringlein, and Jason Haddix for reading various versions and fragments of this text. Your input and support throughout this precarious first-book experience was deeply felt and appreciated.

Thanks especially to Saša for enthusiastically talking through many of these concepts with me, and to Jason for being the first of my friends to tell me back in 2013 that I had something worth capturing and sharing.

It's easy to simply stop writing a book and to never go back. And without you two I very well could have.

Introduction

THE "INTERNET OF THINGS" MEANS many different things to many different people, so let's start with what this book is and is not.

This book is not about the transient technical details that will inevitably transition over the next few years. It's early, and there will be countless iterations and battles over standards.

What this book is about is an inevitable IoT that I believe isn't just a technology upgrade, but a humanity upgrade.

There are three central themes throughout: *prediction*, *interface*, and *evolution*.

Prediction argues---against common opinion---that it is possible to see what technology will look like even decades into the future. It's not that I can tell you all the forms water could take (that's insanity), but what I *can* tell you is the shape of a pothole in a rainstorm.

Interface describes how our interactions with technology are about to become fundamentally less tech-centric and more natural and focused around the human.

Evolution discusses the discussed technologies' ultimate form and function, its value to humans, and the effect it will have on society.

It's a short book, made up of around twenty micro-chapters of one to three pages. Each one introduces a single, discrete concept and has a numbered summary that captures the key points.

You can easily read the whole thing in one session, and when you're done I believe you'll have a unique view into the inevitable intersection between technology and society.

I'm aware of the strength of that claim, so let's get started.

Prediction and Trends

BEFORE WE DISCUSS THE MAIN concepts, I want to call out a number of technological and civilizational trends that are useful to notice and observe. While the forces are somewhat independent, they often interact with one another, and when grouped together they can show us a great deal about where we're going.

First, you might still be stuck on the massive claim made in the introduction.

Is this guy really so arrogant as to think he can predict technology decades into the future? Only geniuses and fools attempt this, and most who think they're the former are actually the latter.

I hear you, and I agree. When I hear crazy long-term predictions I always think two things: either the prediction is going to be obvious, or it's going to be wrong.

I think my approach is different in a subtle and powerful way. Rather than predicting the exact form, of the exact tech, in the exact order that it'll emerge, I'm taking a reverse engineering approach.

Specifically, instead of starting with tech and seeing where it's going, I'm starting with humans and what they seek, need, and desire. In other words, I think we can predict the future of technology through a strong understanding of what humans ultimately want as a species.

So if you want to know the shape of water---which can take any shape---your strongest play is to study the shape of the potholes (and other containers) it'll end up in.

To that end, humans have always sought forms of the following:

* enjoying friends and family

* telling, or listening to, a great story

* falling into, and enjoying, romantic love

* having children and seeing them thrive

* creating useful and/or beautiful things

* becoming more socially influential

* receiving attention and praise from others

* becoming more powerful

These were fundamental human desires 100,000 years ago, and they remain so today. So that brings us this question:

How do we maximize these experiences and capabilities within us, both at an individual level and at the level of society?

Answering that question is the ultimate purpose for technology, and the following trends are some of the forms that this change will take.

FROM CENTRALIZED TO PEER-TO-PEER

We're moving from a world of proxies and mediators to a world of direct interactions. They may use a platform, but the interactions are increasingly between individuals rather than from individual to broker and broker to individual. Not only are direct interactions more efficient, they reduce the opportunity to control others by limiting their access to services.

FROM FORCED TO NATURAL

Because we as humans are still fundamentally what we were on the African plains, technology interfaces that flow naturally with our human intuitions and behaviors will dominate those that require superfluous, foreign actions to work. Expect technological interfaces to move steadily towards thinking, speaking, gesturing, and otherwise emoting, as these are the most human of all behaviors.

FROM OBVIOUS TO INVISIBLE

Technology that distracts from thinking, speaking, and emoting by being obtuse or otherwise distracting will lose to technologies that are invisible. Expect to see technology disappear to whatever degree possible based on current advancement.

FROM MANUAL TO AUTOMATIC

Some tasks are manual and can give pleasure in their execution, such as cooking or tending to a garden. Other tasks are tedious and without redeeming qualities. Expect all such tasks, such as paying bills, handling insurance, driving to work, keeping ones' living space clean, etc., to be handled by technology.

FROM PERIODIC TO CONTINUOUS

Many activities only happen periodically because they are resource (time, money, attention) intensive to execute. These include: assessing the value of assets, adjusting insurance rates, checking the health and happiness of various groups, etc.

FROM PRIVATE TO OPEN

Private information is sensitive because it is private. A natural way to reduce the sensitivity of data (and therefore the risk associated with its loss and misuse) is to have the data become more public in nature. This will mostly take place on its own simply because 1) the value and scale of private data usage in thousands of connected systems and companies, 2) the lifespan of sensitive data (D.O.B/Address/etc.) is much longer than is practical to rotate, and 3) the fact that it's easier to add data to the public knowledge store than it is to remove it.

FROM VISUAL TO MULTI-SENSORY

While visual and audible inputs are the most natural in terms of interacting outside ourselves, we should expect the use of touch and smell to be incorporated into more and more interfaces. This will happen simply because they provide additional native bandwidth into the brain in a way that can be both rich and subtle at the same time.

FROM AGGREGATED TO CURATED

Information services were initially focused on providing as much data to the user as possible because we were information starved. Now the problem is the opposite: Instead of needing more information, we are now overwhelmed by it and are instead in need of filters. The trend, therefore, is to move from raw information being provided to the user, towards the data being processed and tailored by services that produce relatively few curated results.

FROM DESIGNED TO EVOLVED

Perhaps the apex of all trends, this deals with the transition from design to evolution, or from top-down to bottom-up. It's from small numbers of ideas pushed downward by small numbers of people, who think they know best, to large numbers of ideas combined, mutated, and spread laterally and upward by everyone.

The primary benefit of this shift is that ideas will have significant variation and will be free to combine and then be tested as viable solutions to problems. When this combination, mutation, and testing of ideas is performed continuously we end up with infinitely more chances to fail and adjust the approach, ultimately leading to superior outputs.

Many of the concepts discussed starting in the next section will vibrate at the frequency of one or more of these trends.

Universal Daemonization

THERE CURRENTLY ISN'T A GOOD way to maintain real-time information about objects in the world.

The way it's currently done is indirect in a way that will seem primitive once we leave it behind. If you want information about a human, for example, you can't contact the human directly. Instead you need to contact assorted third-party collections of information about them, and basically cobble together a best-case view.

Where is that data located? Hard to say---could be lots of places. What format is it in? Many options available there too. When was it last updated? That varies. How accurate is the information? Well, that'll require research to determine.

It's gross.

The eventual and forthcoming solution is to have information about objects emanate from the objects themselves. The centerpiece of evolved information architecture will be to have objects serve (or appear to serve) as their own sources of truth, with what I call a daemon (DAY-mun) serving as the interface.

All objects will have these daemons. Cars, houses, buildings, cities, businesses, etc. Objects will conceptually emanate their daemons from their physical locations, like a broadcast. Sometimes this will be associated with actual local and physical signals, but will usually be handled through precise online geolocation.

People will interact with objects through their daemons, which will be fully functioning interfaces that allow you to push and pull information as well as modify configurations and execute commands. In traditional computer terms, objects will have universally understood---and functionally comprehensive---APIs.

Daemons will first come to large objects, but will be useful for increasingly smaller, more granular, and more conceptual objects over time. Park benches, trees, sofas, clothing, etc. Physical objects will be obvious enough, but the subsequent step will be to add daemons to conceptual and virtual objects as well, such as businesses, contracts, applications, operating systems, relationships, etc.

The remarkable thing about these daemons is that the technology that will be used to build them is already quite common and available. These are technologies such as TCP/IP, IPv6, HTTPs, and RESTful services. Daemons will be very much like web services technology, which millions of developers already know how to use.

So this is the first building block: every object has a daemon---An API to the world that all other objects understand. Any computer, system, or even a human with appropriate access, can look at any other object's daemon and know precisely how to interact with it, what its status is, and what it's capable of.

Most importantly, humans themselves will also have daemons, and we'll be moving through a world full of other daemons. Human daemons will hold all information about a person, compartmentalized based on type, sensitivity, access restrictions, etc., and that data will be used to send hyper-personalized requests to the daemons around us.

Walking a city block could bring us in contact with hundreds or thousands of them. Every business. Every car. Every person. The street lights, the city cameras, the park benches, the restaurants, the businesses, and the buildings.

Everything will have information and configuration options available, requests we can make, commands we can issue, and it will all be available through standardized protocols and schemas that the whole world speaks fluently.

Summary

1. The future of information architecture is for objects to become authoritative for their own data.

2. Every object in the world will have a daemon that presents itself in a common, transparent, and universally accessible way.

3. Daemons will be fully interactive, with the ability to learn about the object as well as interact with and/or control it.

4. The protocols for building and using the daemons will be standard across the world.

Realtime Data

PERHAPS THE BEST WAY TO think of a daemonized world is to imagine a fabric of interactive and interconnected nodes made up of every object.

Then imagine each of these nodes having instant access to the state of every other node in the fabric. Except it's not just knowledge of state, but the ability to modify, adjust, and command those nodes based on needs, desires, and access.

The power of this should not be underestimated.

Unbelievable amounts of waste can be attributed to imprecise guesses about the state and nature of reality. How far is that city? Is that person married or single? How many people do I know within two city blocks? How many devices are plugged into power on this city block? How happy is this country compared to that one, and what are the factors for that difference?

These are ephemeral truths that have always been to us for any given moment in time because the fact's lifespan has always been shorter than its acquisition period. Stated differently, it always took so much time and resources to learn this information, assuming we knew enough to ask the question correctly from the beginning, that it would often be stale by the time it was gathered, making the whole effort a waste.

When objects maintain their own precise, authoritative, and real-time state, and when that information is available to every other object in the world in a fraction of a second, our connection to reality changes dramatically.

At that point, sensors simply become inputs for realtime data streams published through daemonization. This includes sensors for: light, sound, heat, vibration, chemical composition, EM/RF energy, etc. Cameras and microphones (light and sound sensors) will be the most powerful and prolific of these, and they'll be transformed from hardware used by applications to sensors used to supply data to algorithms.

We learn about the world through analysis of data. We use machine learning and other types of Artificial Intelligence to look at data and give us answers to interesting questions, as well as, to help us ask better ones.

This will be done through a hybrid of local and global resources as is required by the particular application. Certain real-time applications will require instant responses and won't have time to go to the network and back, while others will not have such constraints.

[NOTE: I prefer the term "synthetic" vs. "artificial" intelligence, as its capabilities will end up being just as real as our own despite having non-biological origins.]

But the problem will continue to be the collection and curation of that data. What daemonization provides is an infinite stream of data coming from the sources themselves, i.e., trillions of objects telling you their exact state at every moment---constantly.

Think about universal interfaces between data analysis algorithms and the sources of data they consume. Think about every object's data being presented in a way that natively facilitates continuous data analysis at scale.

From the practical, "What percentage of moving vehicles in Colorado currently have more than two people in them?", to the specific, "Which top three factors most caused unhappiness in the city of London within the last 24 hours?" The point is not any particular query, but rather that we'll be able to ask nearly *any* question and almost instantly know the answer.

When combined with Synthetic Intelligence powered continuous analysis, this is not just game-changing---it's civilization-changing.

And that's just the *reading* part of daemon capabilities.

SUMMARY

1. The lack of realtime data about the world severely restricts our ability to learn about it.

2. Universal Daemonization will provide us accurate realtime data about the objects in our world.

3. This enables sensors (such as light and sound) to continuously feed realtime data into analysis algorithms.

4. This will enable us to have a realtime view of the entire world, constrained only by how much we can evaluate at one time.

Frictionless Interaction

WE'VE SEEN THE BENEFITS OF realtime data for gathering information about the world, but the interactive part of daemons will prove even more powerful. Daemons will likely begin as REST APIs, and all manner of intuitive endpoints will be available depending on the object.

Restaurants will have */information*, and */business*, and */menu*, and */climate*, and */entertainment*, among dozens of others. The parent organization for the restaurant will query the */statistics* endpoint constantly to know exactly how many patrons are present, what they're eating, what they're talking about, which waiters they prefer, which meals they finish and which they don't, etc.

This is not updated every hour or every day---it's updated many times per second as interactions from other daemons within the restaurant stream in.

So when a customer wants to order, they (actually their assistant) will do so by transparently interacting with the restaurant's */menu* endpoint. When it's time to pay, it'll be done automatically via the */payment* endpoint. If they want information on what's showing on the displays, or who the waiters are, or what type of live music will be here this week, they can get all of that easily from the daemon as well.

The same will apply to vehicles and people and cities, with endpoints such as */routes*, and */preferences*, and */population* as respective examples.

This is all powerful, but there's a problem. What are we as individual humans supposed to do with these thousands of daemons that constantly surround us? How can we possibly parse all that information and make use of it, let alone manage all the requests we'll be submitting on our own behalf?

We can't really. That's what Synthetic Intelligence is for.

Summary

1. Daemons not only enable data gathering about objects, but also the making of requests and other types of interactions.

2. The various intuitive functions of an object will be presented in this way, depending on the type of object.

3. In order to make use of daemonization, we'll need to be SI-augmented.

Digital Assistants

THE MOST VISIBLE AND SIGNIFICANT role that Synthetic Intelligence will play in the near future will be serving as the interface between humans and the world.

To clarify, I don't mean the ever-promised, conscious, and self-improving brand of SI that so much science fiction is based on. The SI I'm referring to I define as:

A computer system that can monitor human context, intentions, and commands, interpret them, and then take action as well as or better than a (human) professional personal assistant.

Whether this comes from extraordinary breakthroughs that result in true SI (however you define that), or a mere combination of clever tricks that can emulate it, matters little.

It's been noted, by many who've entered the upper classes, that nothing magnifies productivity and individual effectiveness more than having a good personal assistant. Personal mobile devices combined with SI will bring this advantage to countless more people through digital assistants, and the benefits will be substantial.

To clarify, it's not simply that digital assistants (DAs) will be intelligent, that they'll know our preferences, and that they'll be able to adjust the world to our liking. What's more significant is that they will do this for us continuously.

The preferences piece is essential, because the better your DA understands you the better it can represent you when making requests on your behalf. Your DA will be essentially bound to your own personal daemon, and it will have access to the most protected information within it. Most notably, your preferences and experiences, which will both be used to help construct the ideal contextual requests on your behalf.

This will change how we interact with everything.

The current model is for you to physically manipulate technology, most of which has widely varied interfaces. So you have to find the interface, learn it, and then (hopefully) start using it in some fairly unique way. Then, when you use a different product or service, repeat the process all over again.

The new model is far more simple: voice, gestures, and text. Voice and gestures are part of our natural human communication paradigm and are thus extremely comfortable already, but text has arguably become (for a large portion of the population) a new equivalent of voice. With text you're not learning or using a new tech interface---you're simply "speaking" in a different way and it's the job of the other side to sort out what you meant.

So instead of interacting with technology directly, we will interact with our DA, and our DA will work out the details with the necessary daemon. We speak, things happen. We gesture, things happen. We text, things happen. No need to find, understand, or master new tech---that's for the service and the DA to work out amongst themselves.

What's important is that Digital Assistants will become the preferred interface between humans and the world in a disruptive and foundational way. The idea of having technology that can do something, but that cannot be used perfectly by a DA on your behalf, will soon become extremely uncommon except for specific use-cases.

Summary

1. Daemons are designed to be used by machines, not humans, and the number of interactions required to make them useful will be dozens, hundreds, or thousands per second.

2.   Humans simply cannot (and should not) interact with daemons in this way, and digital assistants using SI will be the broker between us and the technology.

3.   Services (which nearly everything will become) will be designed (and/or retrofitted) to be consumed by Digital Assistants, not by humans.

4.   Humans interact with DAs, and DAs interact with the world.

Tireless Advocate

ONE OF THE MOST POWERFUL aspects of Digital Assistants is that they will be constant and inexhaustible consumers of the world's services on behalf of their principals.

What music should you listen to? What food should you try? Who should you date? In all of these examples there are thousands or millions of options, but your DA can bring that down to one or a few based on its knowledge of you combined with the help of some services that specialize in this. That's curation, and in an environment where there is far too much information for anyone to manage, it's going to become one of the most pronounced benefits to SI-based Digital Assistants.

Think about how much information there is in the world that might help you at any given moment. In books, in articles, in video. In the postings of friends, family, and experts. This will all be harvested for you, while you sleep, while you're distracted, and while you work on other projects.

It's hard to quantify how much value there is for you to benefit from, but your Digital Assistant will work diligently, using all this context, without rest, in multiple concurrent threads, to find everything in the world that could help you in some way. It will then make use of even more services to curate that data for you and then present it to you in the best possible way.

SUMMARY

1. Your DA will use its knowledge of your preferences to be the best possible advocate.

2. Your DA will not sleep, will not rest, and will not get distracted. And it (unlike humans) can actually multi-task.

3. While you are doing other things (or nothing) your DA will be scouring the world for ways to optimize your life based on your needs, desires, and goals.

Augmented Reality

AUGMENTED REALITY IS A PARTICULARLY important addition to the combination of Daemonization and Digital Assistants, as it will give humans entirely new ways of seeing and interacting with the world.

When you look at a strange person in a non-augmented (NAUG) way, you see only what light bounces off of them. You hear only what sounds they can make themselves.

[NOTE: AUG and NAUG refer to whether someone is enhanced or not by a responsive technology system like a digital assistant. AUG is short for Augmented, and NAUG is short for Non-Augmented. The short and/or spoken versions of these (one syllable) are "Og" and "Nog". An example of usage would be to have someone ask after hearing of a high score on a history test, "Wow, was that aug or naug?"]

With daemonization, objects will have extraordinary amounts of data available about them, but, as discussed, humans will be unable to innately interpret that data.

Using the combination of visual, audio, and other sensory enhancement, DAs will use various services (business Daemons/APIs) to create enhanced overlays onto the world. These overlays, or filters, or skins, will communicate context and capabilities available in the surrounding reality that humans would not otherwise be able to see.

Two things are critical for optimal Augmented Reality (AR) experience: Context, and Subtlety.

- With context, DAs will understand the preferences, mood, and intentions of their principals, and they will use this to decide what should be presented to the user through various means, e.g., the visor/lens, temperature adjustments, vibrations, audibly through their earpieces, or even potentially via smell/taste.

- Subtlety refers to how the information is conveyed. It will obviously be possible to overlay giant red text on top of a building that reads "CLOSED", but a simple reddish hue, or a black and white overlay will no-doubt be preferred. Many companies will emerge that excel at producing the best possible experiences of this kind, which will require a combination of creativity, design, and UI/UX expertise.

Now imagine the various contexts that can exist as one moves through life in a given day, and the type of augmented interfaces that can accompany those contexts.

- Looking at a street and having all open shops be green.

- Seeing all highly rated restaurants with a star above them.

- Hearing a musical chime when you talk to someone who is a musician.

- Hearing a backdrop of scary music when you enter a dangerous area.

- Seeing a word cloud on someone's chest representing what others think of them.

- Seeing a truth indicator as a red or green field of vision halo while talking to a stranger.

- Being able to follow a holographic person or familiar/animal as a form of guided walking directions.

- A mood indicator for the room you're in.

- Different music accompanies proximity with people based on their relationship status.

- A Cupid icon floats above romantic matches.

- Best friends or couples who are together are seen with a "besties" or "lovers" label near them.

There will be thousands of these, all made possibly by the combination of these components:

1. Everything is daemonized and displaying data about themselves.

2. Your DA knows your preferences, your current context (happy, lonely, angry, sad, etc.) and is parsing all those daemons.

3. Based on the intersection between those two, your DA uses various AR services (which are business services themselves) to display a contextually rich overlay upon the world.

Companies will specialize, in other words, in making the perfect overlay on a person when they are a romantic match. It's subtle, elegant, and you at once barely notice it and get extreme value from it. And companies will compete to be the AR interface used by DAs for that purpose. And it will be the same for restaurants, detecting danger in an environment, or displaying food on a menu.

The way you see, and can interact with, the world will be constantly augmented in subtle ways based on information your DA knows about you and the environment. And you're not doing anything but going about your day.

Summary

1. Businesses will be competing to artfully display information about reality as AR overlays.

2. These overlays are populated by object daemons combined with the preferences and context of the principal.

3. Your DA determines based on preferences and context which filters to use at any given time.

So with this discussion of Augmented Reality, we've now combined the three core concepts and technologies that make up the main changes to *Interface*:

1. The Universal Daemonization of all objects.

2. Digital Assistants that interact with technology on our behalf.

3. Augmented Reality that adjusts how we perceive and interact with the world based on our preferences and context.

Now let's talk about some of the infrastructure that we'll need to make it all work.

Identity and Authentication

A KEY COMPONENT OF DAEMONIZATION is the fact that each person's (or object's) daemon represents their unique and centralized identity online, and all object daemons are speaking authoritatively as themselves.

So when a DA requests to see products, requests a ride, votes for something, pays for meals, opens doors, or sends a payment to someone, these actions will all come from the centralized identity of the principal that all receiving systems can associate properly. The receiving daemon will then determine whether the requesting entity is able to perform the action in question, and will either approve or deny it.

This is the same way that access is limited to one's own daemon. Only certain people can interact with a daemon to pull information, make requests, etc., depending on the sensitivity of the data/action and the requester's relationship to it. So when someone authenticates to their device---a mobile device for example---they'll be proving that they not only own that device, but also that they are authorized to broadcast and update their daemon as well.

Their DA will then be given access to their daemon, and then they can go about their regular activities.

However, this is going to require a very different approach to authentication.

Right now our identities, and authentication thereof, are handled in a very primitive way. We are who we are because we know something that anyone else could easily know. Or because we have something that anyone else could have. Fingerprints, iris scans, and other types of biometric authentication help, but they don't solve the problem.

The problem is the Last Mile of Authentication, meaning the links between the user, the device, and requests coming from the device, aren't strong enough to enable the kind of functionality that will come with daemonization.

I believe what we're going to move to is continuous authentication, and I think it'll make use of a separate type of service, which I'll call an Identity Validation Service (IVS). And rather than your authentication being based on one thing, or even two or three, it'll be based on dozens or hundreds.

People and things will constantly stream data points to the IVS, and those markers will be used to maintain a real-time confidence rating that the person (or thing) is actually itself. For humans that'll mean you'll be streaming your voiceprint, your fingerprints, the shape of your face, the way you walk, the places you normally are, the sounds in the area, your heartbeat, and dozens of others.

All these flow in constantly to the IVS. Then, when your DA goes to make a request to a daemon on your behalf, it will send your request with a number of signatures. It'll be signed by the device, perhaps some other entities, but *most importantly*, the request will be signed by the IVS. The signature will include a confidence score that---for this particular request, at this particular time---the service is X% confident that it's in fact the right person making this request.

So if someone grabs your mobile device and starts running, they're suddenly lacking wearable input, they're sprinting in a way that's different from you, and when they try to enter a password (which they somehow know) they type differently than you and/or their voice is different. This is all streamed to the IVS (maybe combined with a theft report you just made from your watch), and the IVS is now refusing to sign requests made from that system. Your DA also disassociates from the device.

Additionally, different types of requests will have different levels of sensitivity. Most things you want to do, and that your DA will request for you, will require no additional authentication prompts because your authentication stream and its associated confidence level will be adequately strong. But for certain events, like sending large sums of money, or entering protected areas, your DA might prompt you to authenticate in some way. The requirement will be mapped to the sensitivity of the activity and will depend on how deeply and securely you're already authenticated through your stream.

This is the type of identity and authentication system that will be needed for a daemonized world where your DA is making dozens, hundreds, or thousands of requests on your behalf throughout the day.

SUMMARY

1. Daemonization will require an extremely robust identity and authentication infrastructure.

2. Each object will be presenting authoritatively as itself.

3. Authentication will move from a periodic model to a continuous model, and will make use of an Identity Validation Service.

4. Most authentication will be transparent, but certain sensitive activities will require additional, DA-brokered prompts.

Reputation as Infrastructure

ONCE IDENTITY (SUPPORTED BY PROPER authentication) is thoroughly established, the next thing it'll enable is a rich reputation infrastructure.

Reputation has been a crucial human attribute for thousands of years. Whether you're in a village, a family, or a corporation, your reputation largely makes the difference between opportunity and obsolescence.

Universal Daemonization will greatly magnify the impact of reputation because it will now be global instead of local, and will be validated by third-parties.

This will turn reputation into one of the most important attributes of a person or business, since it'll determine whether someone wants to interact with you or not---as a business, as an institution, and as an individual. Again, it's not actually a new thing. It's been the case since the beginning; it'll simply convert to being represented digitally by being part of your daemon.

Reputation, just as in reality, does not mean just one score. It refers to the multitude of ways that various things are rated, combined with the validation of those ratings by trusted parties.

There will be many types of ratings:

* Reliability at work

* Quality of work

* Attention to detail

* Reliable when friends need you

* Punctuality

* Knowledge of Victorian literature

* Sense of humor

* Attractiveness

* Charisma

* Agreeableness

* Skill with misbehaving dogs

* Attention to detail

* Film sophistication

* Loyalty to employer

* Ability to make complete strangers feel better about themselves

There will be dozens of primary ratings and thousands of subcategories.

One important component of these ratings is that updates to them will stream in continuously from the world. When you make someone laugh, when someone makes comments about you, when you receive a comment on a job you performed, or a performance you gave, etc.

These inputs will be captured by whatever is capable and filtered, interpreted, and weighed by organizations that specialize in ensuring only authentic adjustments are made to your reputation scores. These same companies will then sign/authenticate your scores for consumption, so that anyone looking at the ratings know they are authentic.

Ratings can also appear variably to different people, based on one's weighing of different sources. If someone scores a 79 in Humor, for example, but nine of my closest friends, which I find hilarious, score them at an 85 or above, the score I see may show higher. The same will go for any other rating. Ratings from people you trust, or with similar perspectives, can adjust aggregate ratings.

Most importantly, these ratings will become key attributes of people. They will indicate (with varying levels of accuracy) how smart you are, how funny you are, how reliable you are, how loyal you are as a friend, how attractive you (and others) think you are, how strong you are, quality and level of education, how much money you make, etc.

People will largely control what their daemons are displaying about themselves, so many will choose not to display many things in their daemons, or to only display them to a restricted group of people. But it should fail to surprise that many will display significant amounts of data about themselves.

There are a number of key use cases for these ratings, but one of the most important ones will be the interaction with augmented reality. As people look at other people or objects they will see not just the object itself but information about that object that your DA thinks is most useful at that moment based on your current context.

Your DA may overlay data on an unaltered view of the object, or it may convey the information through modification of the object itself. It could give dangerous people horns, or kind people halos. It could show you highly-rated businesses in color while greying out low-rated options. The options are plentiful and we can expect them to be explored.

Signaling our capabilities to others is one of the most innate and powerfully human behaviors we participate in, we already do this constantly in a myriad of ways. Daemonization and augmented reality will simply make this activity more explicit and accessible.

SUMMARY

1. Our daemons will host and present dozens of ratings (and thousands of sub-ratings) about us.

2. Ratings will be validated by third parties so that DAs, people, and objects viewing your daemon will know which ratings to trust when making decisions.

3. These scores will then be used by the world to make decisions about whether to interact with said person (or object) in various ways.

Continuous Customization

IN ADDITION TO CURATION AND advocacy, digital assistants will also provide another key type of experience enhancement---continuous customization of our environment according to one's desires and preferences.

When you consider all potentially customizable elements of a restaurant, a vehicle, a workplace, a home, or even a city street, you start to realize the impact this will have.

There are two main ways things can be customized, objects themselves can be customizable (e.g., the interior of a piece of furniture, the interior of a vehicle or workplace, etc.)---and you can also customize experiences.

When you enter a resort or a restaurant or something similar, there are countless interactions that actually occur. You have lighting, you have music, you have the appearance and configuration of the interior, and you have the appearance and style of the people you talk to. How does staff interact with you? Are they aggressively taking care of your needs or are they mostly out of sight?

People have different preferences in these regards, and these are preferences that everyone's DAs will have. When you participate in any sort of managed experience (which everything is increasingly becoming) your preferences will be transmitted to the appropriate daemon for customization.

When you enter a sports bar the lighting will adjust, the displays will change to your favorite sport, and a waiter might approach and engage in a style that you prefer (or not at all). Your favorite beverage will be brought to you, your DA will have already consumed the */menu* portion of the restaurant's daemon, and will have options available for you if you ask.

Businesses, buildings, and ultimately every type of object will have an increasing number of configurable options that can potentially be activated according to requests from patrons or anyone where there is mutual benefit.

SUMMARY

1. The world's objects will become highly configurable, with the interface for customization being their daemon.

2. Peoples' DAs will automatically configure physical surroundings, media and displays, as well as overall experiences, for their principals based on their preferences and context.

Algorithmic Experience Extraction

CONNECTING ALGORITHMS TO SENSORS IS going to have a profound impact on how we parse reality, and this effect will be magnified exponentially as people start lifecasting.

Lifecasting, as I wrote about in 2008, is where a significant percentage of the population starts continuously broadcasting what they see and hear. They'll do this to be social with their friends, they'll do it to get famous, they'll do it for practical reasons, and they'll do it for money. It'll simply happen.

What makes it interesting is the combination of these feeds with algorithms.

Humans don't care about video feeds. What they care about are *events*. We want to see first kisses, love triangle fights, humans reacting to new media, car crashes, rescues, heroism, cowardice, and everything in between. We want to see life, and that's precisely what the algorithms will provide us.

As someone goes about their busy day their feed will be monitored and streamed for all manner of events. Aggression, racism, humor, accidents, embarrassment, negligence, wrecks, fights, love, affection, compassion, etc.

When a fight happens in front of someone, for example, the algorithm will clip the video, tag it appropriately, and share it with the appropriate services according to the principal's preferences.

Maybe your DA just sent it to your closest friends, or maybe it sent the clip to a service that pays people for the latest fight clips, passionate kisses, and kindness found in unlikely places.

As a bonus, it also sent a copy to the local law enforcement daemon, and it all happened with no human friction. No clipping, no editing, none of that. The algorithms know when the fight started (the trash-talking, body language, etc.), and it knows when it ended (when everyone fled). It packaged the whole thing up in a fraction of a second, and put a clip in your face and asked, "Should I send it out to these people?" A simple nod was enough.

The same will happen for car wrecks, physical assaults, freak accidents, and any other type of situation where it will be beneficial to have a clean clip of the incident that can be instantly sent to numerous places.

Summary

1. Sensors + Algorithms is a potent combination, as they allow the algorithms to extract meaningful events from life in a continuous and intelligent way.

2. Once those events are extracted they can be shared in countless ways with various services that specialize in or benefit from them.

Omniscient Defender

WE'VE ALREADY DISCUSSED THE CONCEPT of continuous advocacy, whereby the digital assistant is constantly studying the world, curating, and presenting you context-sensitive data that might help you in your life. But there's another use case for your digital assistant being continuously aware, and that's the monitoring of your safety.

Because we're talking about a future of unified identity and ecosystems rather than standalone devices, people will have visual, audible, and other types of access to many places at once. They'll be able to see and hear in and around their home, their vehicles, and any other place that they have extended access to.

This will include networks of monitors controlled by people who've given you access. Your kids, your elderly family, friends, and many others. They could give you access to their personal live stream (when they're not in dark mode or doing something private) so you could see what they see by simply switching to their POV. You could see the environments your children are in, listen to what's going on around them, etc.

Now there are a few reasons why we'd not want to do this. First of all, it's a bit weird to sit and watch everything your kids (or anyone else) are doing just because you could. Second, it doesn't scale. It's hard enough to watch our own live stream (reality), let alone trying to watch your house, vehicles, kids' surroundings, the home of your parents while they're on holiday, etc.

That's what your DA is for.

Your DA will have access to all these systems based on them being either part of your ecosystem, or access being granted by others. So if it's 47 or 470 live feeds, that's fine. Drone visuals so you have overhead views of a plot of land you own? Overhead shots provided by the city of a place where you know you have loved ones? It's all covered.

Why?

Because your DA will watch, listen to, and otherwise monitor all those feeds constantly looking for signs of danger. Is someone moving in a strange way? Is someone following your daughter too close on her walk home? Is their body language similar to that of a purse-grabber or other type of assailant? And if so, what then?

Your DA can do a number of things instantly as a response. It can summon a local private citizen who is in the neighborhood watch to simply come outside and help her walk home. It can call a law enforcement person nearby. It can issue a micro-payment to summon a nearby drone (now enrolled under your DA) and fly over both of their heads while playing Eye of the Tiger or Every Step You Take.

What's so interesting about this is that each stream can have a massive amount of analysis attached to it. Audio streams will go through voice and speech analysis. Your DA will know the likelihood that people are lying around you and your loved ones. The chances that someone in the area is a criminal, or is about to commit a crime, based on body language. Facial and voice recognition.

If you're panicking right now, I am right there with you. It's unbelievably powerful, and the potential for abuse is ruining every chart that tries to measure it.

One concept that you have to keep in mind here is that functionality usually wins over nearly any objection, and the ability to monitor content feeds (visual, audio, RF, air pressure, barometric pressure, chemical air composition, etc.) will simply provide too much benefit for it to not be used at scale.

Thousands of companies will be competing to provide analysis algorithms to look at incoming streams of this data. You simply prove that you're allowed to see the stream, provide access to the company, and it'll give you all manner of live and interesting data about the feed. And where safety is the question, the game will be prediction.

So you'll have access to dozens of your own and your loved ones' feeds, and your DA will be able to monitor them all continuously, using sets of algorithms provided by various companies, paid via micro-payments and subscriptions, that allow you to keep the safety of what you care about within acceptable levels.

SUMMARY

1. Safety is one of humans' most sacred needs and thus will be one of the main applications of technology as it advances.

2. Your DA never needs to rest and will be able to monitor hundreds or thousands of input feeds simultaneously to protect your interests.

3. This monitoring will be augmented by the use of thousands of companies' algorithms for intelligently analyzing the inputs.

4. You will be able to relax knowing your DA is watching what you care about in ways you couldn't hope to.

Human Enhancement

THE COMBINATION OF DAEMONIZATION AND digital assistants will have another application (beyond providing monitoring for safety) that will prove extremely compelling: They will give people extraordinary powers of perception, knowledge, and even action.

As you move through the world on a regular day, your abilities as a human will be greatly enhanced by your digital assistant.

If you are across the street from a building, and there is a visual of the inside of it available, your DA will allow you to look through it. Perhaps like X-Ray vision. Perhaps like thermal vision. Perhaps like you're inside and moving around. But you'll be able to see within as if gifted with extraordinary powers.

When you are looking at a game of Go or Chess, the ideal move---powered by the world's top supercomputers---will be overlaid upon the board as you look at it. Perhaps it will show a green outline of the piece you should move, or give you a lighted arrow showing the path of the piece. It might even give multiple options labeled by what famous players did before in your situation. The AR options are nearly limitless; the key is that you'll be constantly provided with real-time intelligence and curated guidance.

Sitting in a crowded restaurant in Washington D.C., you'll be able to glance at a particular group across the room and indicate that you want to hear what they're saying. All other conversations will fade into a background lull, and you'll hear that group clearly.

When listening to a sales pitch about something that sounds too good to be true, you'll see a meter in the upper left field of view, or an outline around the face of the person you're talking to. It's a visual indicator that will tell you if he is being deceptive or not.

How will your DA know this? Your DA will stream their voice to a business's daemon (or many) that does nothing but rate voices for truth (and other elements). It can tell you if someone is flirting, if they're aroused, if they're angry, or if they're lying. And it gives percentages based on multiple factors (including fact-checking what's being said in realtime).

You'll walk out of a crowded restaurant and ask if anyone was talking about anything interesting in the room, and your DA will give you a three-sentence summary of every conversation you'd probably find interesting.

But it won't just be sound that's enhanced. It will be possible to leverage available cameras to see things with varying levels of magnification and clarity.

If you're in Central Park, for example, and you see a rare bird in the distance. You'll make a gesture and it'll suddenly appear closer and with increasing detail. You'll see it as if you had a powerful telescope perfectly aimed at it. You'll be able to look down at areas from above using the latest available camera, drone, or satellite images.

Your DA will be harvesting all available interfaces to make these views available to you, at all times.

These are not arbitrary features that may or may not be invented. They are guaranteed to happen---and likely early in the cycle of daemonization---because they fulfill a fundamental human desire to become more evolutionarily capable.

Being more aware and more knowledgeable than your competitors is a survival advantage, and these types of capabilities will drive a massive and vibrant marketplace.

Summary

1. One of the most fundamental human desires is to become more knowledgeable and more powerful, as these things are tied to survival.

2. Our DAs will use all resources available to them to provide us with the most and the best possible ways of interfacing with anything we are dealing with.

3. This type of functionality will very quickly spawn vibrant market-places because they appeal so directly to human instinct.

Businesses as Daemons

THE ALGORITHM IS THE CENTERPIECE of expertise. It's ultimately the way of doing something, and that's what makes one offering better than another.

In the past, the core algorithm of a business has been combined with a massive number of other factors to determine success. These include things like having great employees, being in a fortuitous location, or having a given idea at a particular time. As technology connects more and more people to each other and becomes more of the interface to a business, these non-central, non-algorithmic variables will either be removed or will have diminishing effect.

As this happens, algorithm(s) will become increasingly primary to the effectiveness of any given company, and daemons will be the interface that presents that value externally.

Most software businesses will become algorithms presented to others through their business daemons. And many traditional businesses will continue to become software businesses.

Examples will include:

* Finding gifts customized to the exact individual

* Organizing the perfect vacation based on the four people going

* Navigating all the logistics, in the best way possible, of that four-person vacation

- Determining the current mood of a person or a location based on what is known about them

- Finding the optimal route from one place to another, based on the values and states of mind of the various travelers

- Determining the best way to charge a customer based on evolving competition, logistics, and conditions on the ground

All these tasks will be services available online, and there will be several or thousands of competitors in any particular space. There will even be services that consume and rate those services, and present their output (value) through their own daemons.

Many foundational businesses and services will still exist, moving matter from one place to another, the performing arts are an example of this. Some industries and businesses will maintain an analog component simply due to the constraints of physics, but the way they are consumed and marketed will change fundamentally.

CHANGING THE BUSINESS INTERACTION MODEL

One important way this will occur with software businesses, such as retail sites, is through the decoupling of business components that traditionally reside together. Software businesses started as unified experiences: you go to them for the display of the product, you stay with them as you interface with their offerings, and then you use them to pay.

These will soon be separated into discreet pieces. Companies who make things will not be experts in displaying that content to humans. Companies that are experts in UI/UX will not focus on creating content or products. It's specialization, but at an increasingly granular level.

The biggest change, however, will be that the activity itself will be centered around the digital assistant and not with the business.

Users will ask (via voice or text) to view the wares of a business, and this experience will be broken into multiple components. In this example, Sara is working with her digital assistant named Jan.

- Sarah will ask Jan to see headphones from Sequoia (a very popular service for products).

- Jan will contact Sequoia's daemon and retrieve their product list which includes list of recommended UI/UX options.

- Jan notices that Sequoia recommends Ambient's UI/UX filter within the daemon response.

- Jan calls and instantiates the Ambient UI/UX interface and passes the Sequoia product content through it, and then presents that to Sarah.

- Sarah navigates Sequoia's content, using Ambient's UI/UX, using a series of voice commands and gestures.

- Sarah finally says, "This one and this one. Ship to Abdul and Micah. Make sure they're there tomorrow."

- Jan then submits a request to Sequoia's daemon to complete the purchase.

- Sequoia then submits a request to Arrival---their preferred shipping provider, which Jan allows.

The crucial point here is that Sarah spent no time interacting directly with Sequoia's systems.

Jan acted as Sarah's advocate in all of these interactions---retrieving what needed to be retrieved, finding the best way to display it, listening for commands to change the display, and then finally making the purchase and arranging delivery.

The function of the business changes fundamentally in this model. Instead of being in charge of the user's entire experience, businesses become part of an algorithm marketplace used by DAs to satisfy the requests of their principals.

The DA is now the centerpiece of the user experience, and they utilize the services fabric (consisting of business daemons) to choose what will serve their principals best.

Humans make their wishes known and assistants sort out those desires and interact with the requisite services and then present options via a combination of voice, text, and AR interfaces.

Summary

1. Many businesses will become digital and service-oriented because many businesses can (and will) ultimately be reduced to their algorithms.

2. Those algorithms will be presented externally to the world as daemons (APIs).

3. We will interact with our DAs, and our DAs will interact with the APIs required to produce our optimal experience.

The Future of Work

DAEMONIZATION WILL FUNDAMENTALLY ALTER HOW people work.

Businesses will continue shedding human jobs because humans will become increasingly costly, inconsistent, and low-quality compared to algorithms. The future of work is the exchange of value between individuals and groups of individuals, which will become possible with daemonization.

With daemonization you are the source of truth for your own information, and this includes what you're good at. For everything you're skilled in you'll have third-party-validated ratings, and when someone (or more likely their DA) looks at your daemon, they'll know which skills you're competent in, as validated by others (or not if it doesn't matter).

And the same goes for the person requesting the work. They will have been rated by others on how pleasant they are to work with, whether they paid on time, etc.

So the assistants on each side will, using one or more of the thousands of competing matchmaker algorithm companies available, find the ideal match between someone who needs something done, and someone who's able to do it.

At any given moment there are billions of people who need something, and who are willing to pay something for it. There are also billions who have skills and the willingness to help in exchange for something in return.

Daemonization turns work (and value exchange more generally) into a peer-to-peer exchange rather than one mediated by institutions.

So as you're sitting in a coffee shop, your DA will ask and/or present to you through AR, if you want to take incoming jobs. Reviewing a legal document, cat-sitting, talking to a stranger who needs to hear something positive, performing a security audit---whatever. As pre-filtered jobs come in, your DA will present them to you and you can accept or decline them.

But even the word 'work' is a bit limiting. The better way to think about this is value exchange. The fundamental idea at play is that of peer-to-peer exchange and the elimination of the need for institutions in the middle.

Think about other types of services that are currently done by government, such as safety. The future of value exchange has those services coming from peers, not from institutions. If a woman is walking home, and she realizes it's later than she thought, her DA will summon local protection.

People who are rated as safety qualified (large enough to be a deterrent if assisting alone, has training, rated as trustworthy, etc.) will get summoned by their DAs to either accept or reject an urgent, local request. And within a few seconds one or more people will walk up, nod, smile, and walk with her to her destination. Payment could be in actual currency or in appreciation, depending on the transparent and mutual agreement, and the ratings will be logged in the various daemons.

The same might apply for someone hurting themselves and needing help, a child being lost, providing loans, sharing resources, or anything else that a fellow citizen could do faster (and maybe better) than a limited and centralized source of that service.

Those who own particular resources or have particular attributes can make them available to others as part of their value portfolio as well. People who own apartments with a certain view, people who are particularly good looking or charming, people with a sense of humor, etc. You could have the best comic book collection within 50 miles, you could be a highly rated calligraphy instructor, you can have a horse ranch and a bed and breakfast.

People will be able to provide their talents, their traits, their expertise, and their possessions as value to others---all on demand as part of their daemonized value portfolio.

Basically anything you know, are, or have will become experiences you can create and value you can exchange with others. And that will become the new foundation of work.

SUMMARY

1. Businesses would rather not have employees, and they're actively working to discard them.

2. The answer is peer-to-peer exchange of value enabled by matching needs with capabilities.

3. People will provide many such services to each other based on their personalities, skills, and possessions.

4. Daemonization enables the discovery, the vetting, and the coordination of every part of this interaction.

The Four Components of Information Infrastructure

THERE ARE MANY DIFFERENT INFORMATION technologies that will be invented and adopted in the coming decades, but I believe there are four (4) primary categories that they will all fall into.

1. Realtime Data

2. Data Transfer

3. Analysis Algorithms

4. Presentation Interfaces

REALTIME DATA

As I talked about in the realtime data chapter, knowledge of the current state of the world is extraordinarily empowering. It allows us to ask questions about the state of the world and adjust behavior as a result. The more realtime the better, and the more standardized and usable the format the better.

DATA TRANSFER

Now that we have the data available, we need to be able to get it to the algorithms that will perform work on it. The protocols will have to be not only standardized, but built to allow trillions of tiny queries and updates, since even one object's various state attributes could be changing in tens, dozens, hundreds, or thousands of times per second.

Mesh networking will be a significant part of enabling this, as it uses the connections of nearby peers to reach the central network when that otherwise wouldn't have been possible. This is another example of where the peer-to-peer concept will enhance virtually everything.

ANALYSIS ALGORITHMS

Once we have this data the focus turns to the algorithms that will do the analysis. As we talked about in the 'Businesses as Daemons' chapter, companies will largely compete as data analysis algorithms. Companies will largely have access to the same data; the question will be what you can do with that same data that gives you the competitive advantage.

PRESENTATION INTERFACES

Finally we have the output step. We've captured the realtime data, we've moved it to where it'll be analyzed in a standard and efficient way, some company has done their unique analysis on it, and now we're going to display it to someone or something. That's presentation, and it will be another opportunity for companies to differentiate.

Creating the ability to track and present realtime data about objects (and ultimately the world) is hard. That's an engineering problem. The other engineering problem is creating the protocols that will allow us to constantly poll and update objects for their state changes, which will be trillions per second in any large set of objects (like a company, or a city).

Those are efficiency and scalability problems.

The algorithm and presentation steps are significantly more creativity and innovation based. They are ultimately what will differentiate competitors in a long-term business market.

But there will also be innovation in the earlier infrastructure pieces as well, as it's the connective tissue that enables the competition in the spaces of algorithmic analysis and presentation of results.

[NOTE: There is also the option for the output of one algorithm to be sent to one or many others as well, of course.]

SUMMARY

1. Realtime data is collected from the world.

2. The data gets evaluated by algorithms.

3. The output of those algorithms gets presented in some useful way.

4. The collection and transfer of the realtime data are engineering problems, and the analysis and presentation are creative/innovative problems.

Getting Better at Getting Better

ONCE WE ARE POWERED BY realtime data and the infrastructure that makes use of it, the intelligence of our algorithms will become paramount.

Two areas seem particularly promising: machine learning and evolutionary algorithms.

MACHINE LEARNING

Machine Learning is basically the upgrade to our previous-best method of analyzing data---statistics. Where statistics are largely static (the model for extracting truth from data doesn't improve as you add data), with machine learning the analysis actually improves itself automatically.

Machine Learning, in other words, is the ability for computers to learn without being explicitly programmed. And when you apply that to the algorithms doing realtime data analysis of trillions of objects, we can expect the results to be truly remarkable.

We're not just learning about the world; we're improving our ability to learn about the world automatically. And the more data we see the better it gets at improving itself.

EVOLUTIONARY ALGORITHMS

As excited as I am about machine learning, I'm even more excited about evolutionary algorithms---especially when they're eventually combined.

Evolutionary algorithms work by modeling evolution's method of improving things. It has three basic steps:

1. Collect lots of different things together

2. Combine or mate them with each other

3. Introduce randomness into the output

4. Test that output against the environment to see what wins

Another way to say that is:

1. Descent with Modification

2. Natural Selection

That means lots of varied input, combined, random mutation, and then selection of winners.

It's important that you have a good, varied pool to start with. It's also important that you add randomness to the output step so that completely new things are created. And finally, it's crucial that you have a good environment to test in (one that truly represents success or failure).

In nature this is easy---it's just the real world the organism is trying to survive and reproduce in. In the digital world it's a bit more complex.

But the concept is the same, and so is the benefit.

The promise of evolutionary algorithms is that they will allow us to create, very quickly, solutions that human designers couldn't possibly conceive of (and definitely not in that span of time). They work by taking simple inputs, mating them together, adding some random component, and then automatically testing the output to see how successful that generation is. The winners go on and reproduce, with some randomness, and new outputs are tested again.

This is repeated through a number of generations until the line either dies out or something successful is created.

What's so spectacular about this is that with constantly improving hardware, combined with better ways of modeling reality, we can go through thousands or millions of generations of evolution looking for solutions to our problems, all in minutes or hours. Using this technique we can potentially outperform the creative capabilities of billions of the smartest humans, doing their best on a problem for hundreds of years, all in the span of a few hours.

Now imagine that mechanism for improvement, i.e. the one that got single-celled organisms all the way to the point of being able to explore our solar system, and combine that with machine learning algorithms trained to improve the quality of the evolutionary algorithms.

It's difficult to overstate the benefits that can come from being able to accelerate not just our ability to learn, but our ability to learn how to learn. That's precisely what the combination of machine learning and evolutionary algorithms can do---both on their own and when used together to enhance each other.

Summary

1. Traditionally the best method we've had for learning about the world has been statistics, which are largely static; the analysis model doesn't improve when you get more data.

2. With machine learning, the system gets smarter by itself, i.e., without needing to be reprogrammed.

3. Evolutionary algorithms leverage the power of descent with modification and natural selection to create and test possible solutions to problems that we never could as humans.

4. Combining these two---with machine learning improving the modeling and testing capabilities of evolutionary algorithms---may be one of the most powerful advances in technology we'll see for the foreseeable future.

Desired Outcome
Management (DOM)

Now that we've talked about the infrastructure for collecting, analyzing, and presenting information, we can move on to a concept I call Desired Outcome Management (DOM).

The assumption underpinning DOM is the simple claim that we want to improve things but we don't know exactly how to go about it.

DOM provides a model for improving almost anything, and data plays one of the central roles.

DOM is broken into a few main components:

* *Define your goals.* This could be for a business, a city, a family, a department, a country, a team, or an individual. Examples are things like: graduate from a top-10 university, make 100K/year, reach the top 10 ranking in quality of life, attain 150K in passive income, have a happy and fulfilled family, etc.

* *Define your model.* A model in this case is a method or approach for attaining a goal or set of goals. For example, if you want to live a fulfilled life, there might be a Tony Robbins model, or a Dr. Phil model, or a model you make for yourself. It'll have statements in it like, "You need to be healthy to be happy. You need to exercise. You need to eat plenty of raw foods, etc."

* *Capture data.* From there, you need to capture data about your entity's behavior, from the real world, and get it into the system. So if you have a model that talks about diet, you need inputs regarding what you eat, how much you exercise, etc. If your model cares about grades in school, you need to get those grades into the system.

* *Provide Ratings.* Next your system needs to provide clear ratings on how you're doing in the various areas you've chosen to monitor. I prefer A through F, but you can use anything you want as long as it's both clear and simple. Ratings will also include a composite, overall score for your progress vs. your goals.

* *Provide Recommendations.* Finally, the system tells you exactly what to do to improve your ratings in the various areas and overall. So if you're tracking health, for example, and you have a C in activity because you've been sedentary, the system will tell you what to do to improve it. It'll give clear and prescriptive advice, such as, "Row 500 meters, do one set of push-ups, and one set of sit-ups every morning." If you're working on building a great team, the advice after a bad rating might be, "Have more frequent team meetings, and focus on building trust through reduced competitive focus."

* *Adjustment.* The last component of the system is the means by which the model can be updated. Updates to the system come in the form of modifications to the model. This can be addition, subtraction, or changes in importance for elements under consideration. For example, if you're tracking a family's health and happiness, a new study could come out that says shared laughter is crucial to individual happiness. This will be incorporated into the model and recommendations accordingly, based on the research. Similar adjustments will also be made to the model as new information about the world is made available to us.

The adjustment phase is where algorithms will be so crucial. Using machine learning, evolutionary algorithms, and still-undiscovered AI techniques we will continue to extract increasingly valuable insights from the data we have. And because of our access to realtime data through Universal Daemonization, the data being fed into these models will be continuous and fluid.

DOM is just a methodology---a name for a simple yet powerful concept.

1. Have goals

2. Have an approach to achieving them

3. Bring in data about the world

4. Rate how you're doing

5. Recommend changes based on where you could improve

6. Adjust the approach based on new data

7. (optional and/or occasional) Ensure that your goals have not changed

This is a framework for using technology, data, and science to steward humanity's progress forward.

SUMMARY

1. It's one thing to be able to capture data in realtime, move it around, and analyze it.

2. It's quite another to be able to use that data to power your models for improving outcomes.

3. That's what frameworks similar to DOM, realtime data, and machine learning and evolutionary algorithms will help us accomplish.

Peer-to-peer Value Exchange

WE'VE TALKED ABOUT HOW THE future of work is largely person-to-person interaction mediated by a daemon-powered tech layer, but the peer-to-peer model goes far beyond employment.

What daemonized peer-to-peer really enables is less reliance on centralized institutions.

If you are in need of medical attention and there are 38,761 people within one square kilometer, it may not make sense to call on a centralized authority to provide that service.

What if, upon injuring your leg in an accident, your DA could simply beacon out to nearby people. Less than 90 seconds later someone with the proper training, equipment, credentials, and ratings shows up and provides assistance. A micropayment of currency, appreciation, and a high rating is sent from daemon to daemon and the two people go on their way.

The same will apply to safety. Imagine a woman walking alone in a dangerous area and receiving a notification from her DA:

"It's not safe here. I'm getting you some company."

Within a few seconds she's joined by three other people on the street (outlined in green within her view) who smile and walk with her to her destination. There is another exchange of appreciation, smiles, and/or currency, which is reflected on both sides.

Now think of how this could apply to building homes, providing fresh and healthy food, and many other core human needs. Institutions will still have a role, of course, but we the people are in fact the ultimate institution.

Daemonization will allow us to provide ourselves with what in the past needed to be abstracted. It's bottom-up vs. top-down at the ultimate scale.

SUMMARY

1. Once the peer-to-peer infrastructure is set up for all types of services, people will register all the different ways they can provide value to their fellow citizens.

2. The more core services can be provided locally by people nearby (or globally/remotely where applicable) the less we'll need bulky institutions in the middle.

Details and Examples

EACH OF THE CHAPTERS YOU'VE read so far have introduced a single concept per section. I did this to make the concept crisp and simple, which isn't possible if you start talking about how it might be implemented.

In this section I give a few additional ideas and likely/possible applications for each.

UNIVERSAL DAEMONIZATION

* The more up-to-date an object's information the better, so the informational endpoints will have update/validate options available for external clients that aren't able to make changes to the daemon itself. For example, if a mobile business is marked as being at a certain street corner, but it moves without updating itself for whatever reason, it will be able to accept update requests from people who see that it's moved in the last few seconds.

* State updates of this kind will depend on the authority, reputation, trustworthiness, and how many votes come in that agree. Entire economies will emerge based on paying micro-payments for providing high-quality validation of reality. The status of businesses, the location of common objects, ratings of service, etc. People will potentially make livings by simply observing and reporting state

updates in a responsible and valuable way that are then stored in the objects' daemons.

* Even basic information about an object will have their own meta-ratings that determine how trustworthy they are. Examples will include how often they're updated (per day, per minute, per second, etc.), how many external validations have been made with what authority, etc.

* Daemonization won't be just for physical objects like vehicles and buildings and people. They will also be used for (and useful to) conceptual and virtual objects such as applications, companies, businesses, networks, etc. Think of the use case of an IT asset database, where all applications, servers, operating systems, tests, builds, vulnerabilities, etc.---all have their own daemons and their own realtime status.

* This information architecture makes queries and updates simple and elegant---exactly as they should be. When you run a security scan and find vulnerabilities, they each have their own daemon with their own schema, and they're attached to an application that has its own, which sits on top of an operating system, which sits on a piece of hardware, etc. So finding out what version of software sits on what OS, what data is being used where, how that data is changing, where it's moving---these all become daemon status updates that are available in realtime.

* There will be complex infrastructures built for filtering and vetting of incoming requests to daemons for the purposes of confidentiality, integrity, and availability. This will focus heavily around who is able to see what, who is approved to use specific daemons in what ways, and countering attempts to spoof, hijack, or otherwise compromise peoples' identities.

REALTIME DATA

* One of the biggest advantages of realtime data will be serving as a constant stream into scientific studies. So rather than data analysis taking days, weeks, months, or years, we'll be able to pull that data every day, every hour, every minute, or multiple times per second, constantly, and at scale.

* Realtime data also allows us to more quickly study the effect of variables in these scientific studies due to the high quantity and quality of data coming in. If we're able to track mood in realtime, for an entire city, then we're more likely to be able to do the regression required to say that a particular variable (or number of variables) was the cause of the change in mood.

* Realtime data will also be able to speak to, at a more granular level, the difference between causation and correlation simply because we'll have more great data to use.

* Ultimately, realtime data is the most important component in the Information Infrastructure and Desired Outcome Management concepts, since it's the data that's feeding the algorithms and output, and the standardized structure of that data will make it easy to consume and use without extensive normalization and massaging.

* People or systems will simply ask questions about the state of the world and get answers, e.g., how many dolphins are there within one mile? Is this area more Star Trek or Star Wars? How many airplanes are there over my head, which country's currency has lost the most value in the last hour, how many single people who prefer cats to dogs are within a 10 minute drive, what's the most popular fast food in this area?

- These types of queries will obviously require the other pieces of the information infrastructure as well (data transfer, algorithms, etc.), but the data is the most important component.

DIGITAL ASSISTANTS

- DAs will basically run our lives, from wakeup time (based on your sleep cycles and the latest research), to which method works best (raising the lights and playing certain music), to starting your favorite food and beverage, preparing to read/display your preferred news sources, etc.

- Your household, work environment, and any other place you spend time in will be run by your DA as the custodian of your life ecosystem, with you as the owner.

- When you buy new equipment it will of course be daemonized, and the enrollment process will involve it being added to your ecosystem. That means it'll be automatically hardened and access controlled based on your ecosystem. So if friends and family can do certain things with certain kinds of devices, but not with others, those settings will automatically apply to this system as well.

- Instead of household items like food and dish soap and paper towels ordering replacements for themselves, i.e., talking directly to businesses, every household item will register with the head-of-household's DA, and the DA will manage the household based on its knowledge of your preferences, calendars, etc.

- Your DA basically manages your ecosystem according to your values and preferences, and any new extension of that ecosystem will instantly be adjusted to behave in accordance with those values.

- Your DA will notify you in certain ways, which will over time produce Pavlovian responses, when certain situations arise. You'll hear a sound when a single person of the opposite sex nears you while you're not working, but only if they pass a few filters that are important to you.

- You might let your DA use a number of commercial algorithms to find matches for you that you wouldn't have thought to explore yourself. So you may put yourself in Cupid mode, or Spontaneity mode, where two DAs create pre-filtered but semi-chance meetings between two people.

- Spontaneity itself will be managed as a life experience setting that your DA can turn up or down. That can apply for food, music, romantic recommendations, news, etc. Curation is fantastic, but the downside is a bubble where you see the same things over and over.

TIRELESS ADVOCATE

- If someone mentions to you casually about a particular sport, your DA (knowing you like to immerse yourself in new hobbies) will find the nearest training locations, the best local trainers, the best and nearest places to play, and some top tips for getting into shape. So when you inevitably ask about it in the next day or so, your DA will have an entire plan sorted out for you.

- Any research topic you express interest in, or ask your DA to look into, will get a full parsing and summary treatment, ultimately resulting in a summary (which probably comes from its own commercial API) that gives you exactly how much information you wanted on that topic.

* Summaries will have depth levels, so you'll be able to say things like, "less depth", or, "more depth" as desired, but that'll only be when it doesn't get it right in the first place.

* DAs will scour the world looking for negative information about you, news that could negatively affect you, etc., and will bring it to your attention if it finds something, along with potential fixes.

* Your DA will constantly review the set of algorithms (companies/ services) it uses to optimize your life, and will make sure it's using the best / most affordable options.

AUGMENTED REALITY

* When speaking to someone either in person or remotely, you will see indicators in your field of vision telling you how truthful they're being. This will be from voice analysis, facial expressions (if it's a visual call), etc. The visual indicators might be a Pinocchio nose, a red outline around them or your field of view, or it may be a non-visual indicator, like a subtle hissing or vibration.

* As you're talking to people you'll have metadata about them displayed, such as humor scores, attractiveness ratings, favorite foods, favorite books, and interesting connections to you like mutual connections, that they attended the same college, etc.

* Single people in public places will automatically see potential matches in different ways, e.g., displaying a cupid over their heads, showing them in color while everyone else is grayed out, etc.

* The context that you're currently in will be explicitly set by you or automatically set by your DA. If you haven't eaten and your stomach rumbles your DA might switch you into "food finding mode", which displays restaurants near you in particular ways based on what you've eaten recently, your favorite type of food, which places have the best ratings, etc.

* Kind people will be able to turn on the Gloomy filter and see a gray and raining cloud over the heads of people who need cheering up.

* You'll be able to see live crime statistics for the area you're currently in whenever it's after a certain hour and you're in an unfamiliar place.

* Companies will specialize in providing artfully subtle yet powerful AR indicators for various contexts, e.g., hungry, lustful, angry, skeptical, curious, tired, frightened, sad, depressed, euphoric. Each of these will have different displays in your visual field, ambient and directional sounds, subtle vibrations in parts of your body, smells, etc.

* Becoming frightened in a strange area could outline everyone in green or red to indicate who to avoid or seek help from based on facial imagery, gait analysis, body language, etc.---all of which is being streamed in realtime to a series of business daemons that specialize in this type of analysis and UI/UX display.

* When people are sad or angry, your DA will stream the situation and the context to a company/algorithm which will display the perfect thing to say to solve the problem. It could be a de-escalation phrase, or a phrase that takes responsibility, or shows empathy, or whatever that situation needs.

IDENTITY AND AUTHENTICATION

* As you move throughout the environment, whether at home or overseas, doors will open or not open based on who you are and what level of authority you have according to that resource. If you're a police officer in the United States, for example, and you are in Munich, you might be granted access to POV access to a certain street camera, while your friend who is not in law enforcement will not.

* When you purchase (or lease) a new object, such as furniture or technology, you'll simply enroll it through your DA into your ecosystem. All of your preferences will be automatically applied to it, including how it's locked down, who can access it, under what circumstances, etc.

* When you sign up for new services and experiences, your DA will transparently convey both your authentication validation (which will be signed by your Identity Verification Service) and all your preferences.

REPUTATION AS INFRASTRUCTURE

* You ask your DA where to go for a weekend trip, and it calculates all the variables based on the best experience, price, and ratings by people in your network who have gone there. Your DA recommends the winner and then uses a separate daemon/business/API to build the travel plan and add it to the calendar.

* There will be algorithms/companies that do nothing but find special combinations of high ratings in random things. Like making people laugh, combined with being able to bake, combined with

cosmology knowledge, and will use this cocktail to recommend relationships or problem-solving connections for people.

* People rated extremely high in altruism and selflessness in terms of actually giving time and resources will be able to soak up micropayments from those around them. I may have a small amount of money that I transparently give to those like that around me, for example, and they might be able to just go through life giving of themselves without worry of where to eat or sleep. It's an extreme case but it will be possible, especially with local businesses helping with free goods.

* People will be more likely to treat others well since they won't want their selfishness ratings to rise too high, which could lead to paying higher prices for things, not getting access to certain places, or people choosing not to interact with them.

* Authenticity will be a primary marker solely to prevent people trying to game the system in a negative way. Both people and algorithms will be good at telling the difference between pretending to care and actually caring.

Continuous Customization

* Walking into a sports bar could see the content on the displays change, the music over the speakers change, etc. You could get one waiter vs. another, be asked about your day or not, have the temperature in the place raised or lowered, etc.

* If you work at a physical location, your settings will instantly transfer, including your desk height and angle, your chair settings, the lighting in your cube, your communication settings, how often you are to be interrupted, etc.

- When you visit a hotel your DA will have everything configured for you according to the maximum capabilities of the property. This will include bed style, products in the bathroom, what's playing on the display, the temperature in the room, etc. These are not things that you ask for---they're all things that your DA knows best about you, and it simply transfers that to the property as a customization package request.

- As you move from place to place (say hotels or airplanes) your context will transfer with you through your DA. If you're halfway through watching a show on a plane when you land, your DA will ask if you want to pick it up where you left off when you get in bed at the hotel.

- Anything that's customizable that you visit will be adjusted by your DA in this way. Walk into a new home dealership and you'll hear your favorite music, or an ideal experience for that environment, you'll get your favorite drink, and someone will interact with you in a way you'll enjoy.

- Customization will include spontaneity, since your previous likes will inevitably get old. Part of your DA's job, as well as the job of various experiences, will be to delight you with new music, new lighting, new interactions, etc. This will be handled through thousands of competing businesses/algorithms/daemons.

- At certain really important times in your life, like when you're out riding bikes with a childhood friend in your hometown, you might both hear a perfect soundtrack of the music you used to listen to together. These are perfectly curated experiences, performed by your DA, using specialized experience companies/algorithms. The purpose of these APIs is to always have the perfect song, or the perfect view, or the perfect whatever, for that situation.

Algorithmic Experience Extraction

- A fight breaks out in front of you and the entire escalation, altercation, and aftermath are sent to local authorities for review before police even arrive.

- You're walking through a field and a massive hawk swoops down and grabs a mouse right in front of you. It's turned into a captivating, professional slow-motion video and is uploaded to a number of nature sites. You receive decent money off of the rights to it for a month.

- A young couple meet for the first time and, algorithms detect that they are likely to go long-term. You send them a curated third-person perspective of the meetup that they can only open if they're together in 5 years.

- A tornado comes through a small town and thousands of clipped experiences are uploaded so people around the world can instantly experience what it was like.

- Something is stolen in a public, visible area that deceived humans but did not deceive your enabled analysis algorithms. A clip of the incident is edited and your DA asks what you want to do with it.

Omniscient Defender

- You'll be notified by your DA if anyone in your family is in a dangerous situation that falls above a certain threshold.

- You'll be able to switch your visual point of view instantly to any camera you have access to, whether that's inside your house, through the eyes of someone you're sharing access with, drones hovering over your house, etc.

* You and your loved ones' DAs will be scanning the environment for situations that seem dangerous. More specifically, they'll be streaming live footage to their preferred company/algorithm that specializes in assigning danger ratings to environments.

* Your DA will stream surrounding conversations to a company/algorithm to alert you of anything that could be dangerous to you.

* Your entire ecosystem becomes eyes, ears, and noses for your DA to monitor your family and possessions 24/7.

* Your DA will let you know when you are being monitored, when you should disable your daemon, take other countermeasures, etc.

* Your DA will let you know when you're doing something that could be controversial, and give you the capture points that it could be pulled from. It will be constantly monitoring ways you could be monitored and make sure that you're not causing harm to your reputation.

HUMAN ENHANCEMENT

* As you move into new areas your DA will query and load up various views of different objects you might look at. So you could look at a building and see the people inside as heat signatures, or you might see the schematics of a building from a distance, all as AR overlays.

- With a gesture or a voice command you will simply enable X-Ray vision, or heat signature, and then see the world through that perspective. Things that were pre-loaded will show quickly, others will take time, and others will not show at all because there's no data for them. But over time, and with enough daemon access, we'll be able to see much of the world in this way.

- The same will apply to hearing, with the ability to focus on someone across a parking lot and hear what they're saying. You'll be able to gesture, target, or do some other aesthetically appealing way to initiate and visualize the effect. When it kicks in you'll hear the person talking as if they're speaking in your ear.

- You'll be able to zoom into things visually as well, and things you can do this with will be subtly indicated within your AR interface, perhaps with a tiny telescope in the top right corner. For any of those items you can make a gesture and zoom in and out using whatever nearby cameras that exist (that you have access to).

BUSINESSES AS DAEMONS

- Play the perfect song for this moment.

- Find the perfect gift for this person.

- Write the perfect letter for this situation.

- Create the perfect song for this situation.

- Give me the best path from A to Z given this cargo and time of travel.

- Display this content to me in the way that will help me make the best decisions in the least amount of time.

- What should I watch right now?

- When I look at the cover of a book, give me a perfect summary that fills the cover, along with the rating.

- What should I listen to?

- Why am I not happy?

- If I redesigned my living room, what are the top best options?

- What do I waste the most time on in my life?

- Surprise me with an interesting music choice that I'll love but never would have picked myself.

- Remind me when there's someone I care about that I haven't told how much I love them.

- Show me how much danger I am in at any given moment.

- Show me the local crime statistics for the area I'm in.

- Spend up to 5,000 to automatically deploy local defenders if anyone in my family gets in danger.

- Only show me menu items that I should eat as part of my new health plan.

- Build me a perfect daily routine based on my life goals.

- Find the perfect girl for me.

- What comic series would I like?

- I'm new to Sushi, what should I try on this menu?

- I just got this text, how should I respond?

- I need to impress this person I just met; build me a weekend spending no more than 1,000 that they'll love.

- Who's hurting the most within 1 mile, and what can I do for them?

- For every neighborhood in every city, establish baselines for customs, behavior, etiquette, etc., so that you can be notified if people are behaving abnormally in a way that indicate danger.

THE FUTURE OF WORK

- Jason is rated highly in many local and global skills, and he sits relaxing at his favorite coffee shop. He's asked his DA to only bother him with incoming job requests if they pay over a certain amount. Because of his high ratings in these skills, he often gets fiction editing requests, requests to help move things, cat-sitting, legal contract review, and empathic listening. When a job passes the threshold, his DA (named Timothy), will break in quietly in his earpiece. "Legal contract review, 37 pages, due by tomorrow morning, are we interested?" Jason nods his head and the details are worked out between DAs transparently.

- Nadia sits at her favorite co-working location watching incoming job requests scroll by her AR display. She's a coder so she's watching the logos for various languages scroll by, with the size of the icon representing the payment for the project. She also gets lots of requests for helping people with programming, which she sometimes takes just to be nice, since they don't pay much. She sees a big project in her favorite language scroll by and tells her DA (Vira), "I'll take that one."

* Companies will specialize in finding better matches of job seeker and job taker based on hidden truths they extract using their proprietary algorithms.

* You'll be able to simply say, "Find me someone to help me move this pile of rocks," or, "Find me the best person to edit this photo." Your DA will contact multiple companies/algorithms to find the best fit for you (if it doesn't know already) and that company will connect you with the best service or person.

* You'll be able to specify that you prefer local, that you prefer in person, that you prefer best in the world, that you prefer cheap, etc. And the algorithms your DA uses will take this into account.

The Four Components of Information Infrastructure

* There will be countless companies competing to provide various parts of the sensor, daemon, transfer, algorithm, and interface infrastructure. They will be modular in nature so that one company's sensors can interface cleanly with another company's daemon technology.

* Each piece is a bottleneck to the entire system, so realtime data for increasingly large systems (consisting of billions and trillions of

nodes) will become possible as the minimum capacity component in the infrastructure is upgraded at any given time.

+ Mesh networking will become an absolutely revolutionary component of the information architecture, and the concept ties heavily into the peer-to-peer magnifier. People who cannot connect to the greater network might be able to connect to one or more people near them who can, and this mechanism will be used to exponentially increase the number of people who can stay connected at all times.

GETTING BETTER AT GETTING BETTER

+ As algorithms start replacing humans, the pace of improvement will only increase. We'll see it in algorithms getting better at handling customer service issues, driving, obtaining knowledge, etc. The advantages of these gains can be almost instantly transferred and applied elsewhere in the industry and instantly spun up. Alternatively, human workforces constantly need to be created, trained, and re-trained due to churn.

+ Machine learning and evolutionary algorithms will be used to improve each other, accelerating the pace at which both can improve.

DESIRED OUTCOME MANAGEMENT

+ Algorithms will be pointed to realtime datasets that are continuously updated, and the algorithms will continue to optimize themselves as they consume more data.

* Philosophy will become far more interesting because once the data infrastructure is more standardized and modular, the value from data, statistics, and machine learning will increasingly hinge upon asking the right questions. The right questions, in turn, will hinge upon our goals and will unfortunately require philosophers to help figure out (and articulate) what those should be.

Peer-to-peer Value Exchange

* Eventually people will build communities that are functionally, emotionally, and economically tied to each other through mutual dependence and support. Value exchange, providing of services, infrastructure mechanisms, etc.---will all be handled internally to a significant degree in order to return to a sense of nature and local lifestyle.

* Fewer services (but still many) will require centralized, institutionalized resources, as the peer structure will eventually be robust enough to handle most needs. Exceptions to this norm will be in the areas where it makes sense, construction and emergency vehicles for example, to have a permanent staff available at all times.

* People will supply each other with conversation, food, recipes, storytelling, security services, medical services, empathic listening, art critique, physical labor, etc. The tech will enable the human elements.

SUMMARY OF CONCEPTS

WE COVERED A LOT OF ideas here, so let's just review the main points.

- There are basic trends in technology that we can see crystalliz-ing: centralized to peer-to-peer, forced to natural, obvious to in-visible, manual to automatic, periodic to continuous, scheduled to realtime, private to open, visual to multi-sensory, aggregated to curated, and designed to evolved.

- Objects, including humans, will become their own authoritative sources of truth for information about them through a concept called Universal Daemonization.

- Universal Daemonization will allow for realtime data gathering about objects in the world at nearly any scale.

- Daemonization will be bi-directional, allowing for the updating of, pushing to, and issuing of commands to other objects.

- Because humans will not be able to parse and interact with bil-lions of daemons, Digital Assistants will perform this task for them.

* Digital Assistants or Advocates (DAs) will work to optimize the life of their principals continuously, without rest, 24/7/365, and in multiple threads.

* Our DAs will use AI to subtly alter their principals' interface to the world, giving them better knowledge and providing interfaces for modification.

* All requests made from your daemon will be made as a centralized identity, and third parties will validate that it was truly you that made those requests.

* Our daemons will display numerous reputation scores about us which are also validated by third parties.

* Our DAs will constantly customize our experiences around us by modifying what things look like, how they're configured, and how we experience them, through transparent daemon interaction.

* Constantly improving algorithms will be connected to the billions (then trillions) of sensors in the world, and they will constantly parse reality into events and data that are meaningful to humans that can then be shared with various entities.

* Our DAs will use whatever resources they have (thousands of eyes and ears) to monitor us, our loved ones, and our valuables for safety and security.

* Our DAs will functionally grant us superpowers through the enhancement of our sight, hearing, and many other sense types that we don't even naturally possess.

* Businesses will become daemonized forms of their core algorithms, and the primary consumers of these business daemons will not be humans themselves, but rather their DAs using the services on behalf of their principles.

* People will broadcast their third-party-validated capabilities through their daemons, and this peer-to-peer infrastructure will represent the future of finding and securing work.

* The four ways of gathering and using data will be: realtime data from objects, transferring that data, analyzing the data using algorithms, and then presenting it in some useful way.

* The combination of machine learning and evolutionary algorithms will not only improve our ability to learn about the world, but will improve our ability to improve that ability.

* This will culminate in a framework that allows humankind to systematically define its goals, study reality in realtime using AI, and then make optimizations to our behavior that best lead to our desired outcomes.

* Daemonization will ultimately allow humans to reduce their reliance on large, abstracted institutions and instead look to each other for their needs.

WHAT DOES IT ALL MEAN?

So we've talked through the various concepts. But what does this all get us? How is this the future of technology and humanity?

There have been three main themes throughout this book:

1. That we can predict the future of technology through our understanding of what humans ultimately want as a species.

2. That human-to-technology interface is about to fundamentally change by abstracting technology behind natural interfaces.

3. That we're moving towards a bottom-up and evolution-based model vs. one that's top-down and design-based.

PREDICTION

We cannot know what technology will be capable of in the future, but the more we understand ourselves the more we will know exactly how it'll be used. That dynamic is the key to our predictive power.

We are the imperfect pothole, and technology is the puddle inside. Know the shape of the container and you'll know the shape of what fills it.

Given that perspective, technology is perhaps best defined as:

An artificial layer of abstraction that converts an entity's desire into reality.

Technology is what fills the gap between the world we have and the world we want, and in that sense it is far more predictable than most realize.

INTERFACE

With regard to interface, the future of technology is one where technology usage becomes more natural, more invisible, and completely abstracted. Poking at applications applications with fingers or keyboards is identical to running clothes up and down a washing board---in a river.

We're not just moving to a model where humans interact with their computers via voice, text, and gestures---that's a small detail in the larger point.

What we're moving toward is a model where humans don't really interact with computers at all. Instead, humans will interact with assistants who then interact with computers on our behalf. It's mediation. It's abstraction. It's humans simply wanting or needing things, naturally communicating those needs implicitly, or explicitly, and having those things simply happen.

The world becomes transparently curated and reconfigured around us according to our preferences.

EVOLUTION

Finally, daemonization will unify a person's identity into a single source of truth that lives where it should: *with you.*

Instead of being the fleshy, abstracted subject of thousands of imperfect databases, you will become the single authority for who you are, your realtime state, what you care about, and how you prefer to interface with everything else.

It will allow us to know the state of the world in realtime, to parse that information continuously, and to use technology to shape our lives according to our values.

This not a technology upgrade, it's a humanity upgrade.

It's knowledge of, and connection with, all other objects through our respective daemons---allowing you the ability to create and exchange value in realtime.

It will transition us from a model where institutions slowly and imprecisely interact with other institutions about us, to a model where we interact and exchange value with each other.

This is the real Internet of Things.

AFTERWORD

THERE ARE MANY WHO WILL read this book and see nothing but dystopia. In certain moods, I'm one of those people.

What's important to understand, however, is that I'm not conjuring this reality into existence. I'm not enabling it to happen. I'm simply describing what is---without question---*going* to happen. As I talk about in the initial concept of Prediction, these are things that will come to pass not from conscious, planned thought, but rather because this is what humans will demand---and inevitably receive---because of what our species innately desires.

The amount of functionality these technologies will bring, and the demand for them by both consumers and industry, will be too powerful to oppose. They are an arriving train, and all we can do is get ready for it. When it gets here, it might run us down or it might take us comfortably to our destination. But it's coming either way.

Many of the possible uses for these ideas deeply trouble me. As someone who cares about inequality, I see DAs as powerful levers for the successful to pull even further away from the masses. As someone in cybersecurity, I have compiled my own personal legion of abuse cases for so many of these capabilities, and they range from the troubling to the terrifying.

But my distaste for, and concern about, many of the potential abuses will not stop me from either alerting people of what's coming, nor from seeking a way to transform it into something positive.

Hating the thought of this tech harming our humanity is natural, but don't allow the unpleasantness convince you that it isn't there, or that it isn't inevitable. It *is* there. And it *is* coming.

So let's use our energy to make the arrival as safe, secure, and beneficial to humanity as possible. Denial and dismissal help no one.

EXTENDED CONTENT

THERE IS FAR MORE TO say on each individual topic presented here, as well as more topics to add. As I do I'll be capturing them on my site at: danielmiessler.com/blog/. Please join me there as I continue to explore the concepts with related ideas, additional use cases, and conversation about how these technologies can and will be misused.

danielmiessler.com/blog/

COLOPHON

- San Francisco CA, London UK, Newark CA

- 2016

- macOS Sierra

- Vim

- Markdown

- Pandoc

- Zomby, Glitch Mob, Technoboy, Ratatat, Cryptex, Behemoth, Opeth, Gojira

Made in the USA
Middletown, DE
20 March 2018